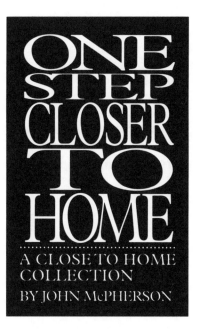

ONE
STEP
CLOSER
TO
HOME

A CLOSE TO HOME
COLLECTION

BY JOHN McPHERSON

Zondervan Publishing House
Grand Rapids, Michigan

A Division of HarperCollins*Publishers*

Published in cooperation with Zondervan Publishing House.

Library of Congress Catalog Card Number: 94-71740

ISBN: 0-8362-1764-0

For Mom

"This isn't what I was expecting when they asked us over to see their slides."

"You want your dessert now or later?"

"Wow! That was neat, Dad! OK, teach me how to throw it! Dad?!"

"Watch your step going through the living room. Lloyd got a little confused when it came to installing the new ceiling fan."

Ted felt it was important to have a résumé that would catch the personnel manager's eye.

"My typewriter broke, so I had to do my term paper on the Etch A Sketch."

Losing the TV remote control awakened Bob to the fact that he wasn't exactly in peak physical condition.

"Don't be too impressed. It's not real. My kid made it out of Legos."

"Wonderful. We spend $200 on toys and she plays with a shoe box
for three days nonstop."

"They say that having a new baby in the house can be very traumatic for pets, so to help the cats adjust, we've been rubbing catnip on Mikey."

"Vern considers it a sign of weakness if he empties the grass bag before he's finished the lawn."

Norm Pitloff would go to any length
to use the car pooling lane.

"I don't think you need to push quite so hard, Dad."

"I'm saving up to get one of those
jogging treadmills."

"I thought the tassel looked a little bland
so I had it permed."

Many first-time fathers take the job of videotaping the birth far too seriously.

As a courtesy to their fellow joggers, more and more people are starting to wear mudflaps.

"This darned icemaker is on the fritz."

Where doctors keep their stethoscopes.

**Vern had yet to master the art of first-date
conversation.**

"Thank heavens this vacuum has a reverse button!"

"Sorry about that little power outage there. We were installing an electric air freshener in the men's room. Hope we didn't mess up yer data or whatever yer doin' there."

"That's one of the things about living in an old house that drives me nuts. Never enough outlets."

20

Once again, Wendy beats her curfew.

"For cryin' out loud, just pick one! He's never going to recognize it!"

"My baby-sitter's got the flu."

"I liked it better when it just beeped when we were overdrawn."

"This'll be a good chance to test that rustproofing job on the car, huh, Dad?"

"I thought you said you fixed the problem with the blow dryer."

Get even with guests who snoop in your medicine cabinet. Fill it with marbles before your next party.

"I guess maybe *now* my canine ankle fences don't look so stupid, huh, wise guy?!"

How to humiliate your husband

"Remember the good old days when they were all just called 'sneakers'?"

"I hope this is just some kind of cruel joke, Dad!"

Budget stress test

"Maintenance says they'll be here first thing tomorrow. They're tied up fixing a leaky toilet over in personnel."

"Oh, look at this! Our little girl coming home from her first date! You kids just go ahead and say good night as though we're not even here!"

29

"I want to start getting used to this backpack
before the baby comes along."

30

"What are you mad at me for? He loves this! Plus this terry cloth outfit he's wearing is perfect for waxing the car."

"Sorry about this. My mom's a little bit paranoid
when it comes to stuff like sparklers."

"I think you missed a spot with the sunscreen."

"Did somebody here call about too much air conditioning blowin' on their head?"

**Unable to decide on a name for their baby,
Steve and Kim Robb leave it to fate.**

**"Hey! I'm picking up another strong signal here!
Gotta be at least a half-dollar! Heh heh! We need to
have the Schmitts over more often!"**

"Can you feel the Novocain yet?"

"Elaine's been bugging me for years
to give her more closet space."

"Hey! You're right! They *are* big jelly beans."

"Well, we hope you slept good. Believe it or not, we picked that sofa bed up at a garage sale for only $50!"

"Looks like I better switch and start using *this* arm to hit the snooze button."

"For total biking realism, here's our finest exercise bike, complete with a growling dog, a tape deck that plays rude comments from motorists, and this nozzle which emits a fine mist of bugs."

"As most of you know, the company has undergone cutbacks recently."

"You can come out now, Mrs. Ziffler. Ron caught Howie and locked him in his room. Say, if you're free Friday night, we'd love to have you baby-sit again."

Lisa's dad had a surefire method for getting her downstairs in time for dates.

Chuck and Pete don't let the fact that they live in Kansas stop them from experiencing the thrills of surfing.

"Be sure to compliment him on his wife and kids."

"Why on earth can't you learn to pull up closer?!"

"Granted, it doesn't have the versatility of our other models, but most people find it much easier to play."

"He drank the last cup of coffee and didn't make a fresh pot."

"Are you trying to destroy my social life?
I know people around here, Dad! Please take off
that stupid hat!"

"How's the wild rice?"

"Get the red Buick in the third row."

"This stupid thing is clumping up again."

"I forgot to peel the labels off our glass jars and bottles."

The ever-annoying Naugahyde-in-summer syndrome.

"Phil did all of the plumbing in the house entirely by himself."

"This isn't what I had in mind when I requested a semi-private room."

There are times when being a whiz at physics
can be a definite drawback.

Fortunately, Eleanor was able to get a full refund from the computer dating service.

"Jerry, the Morrison kid is here. He wants to know if we offer a health plan in addition to the five bucks we're paying him to mow the lawn."

Even though they were hard to run in, Don's new shoes made him a serious base-stealing threat.

After spending $30 a square yard for new carpeting,
the Schindlers weren't taking any chances.

It was only July, but already the dreaded signs began to appear.

Despite the popularity of biking shorts, only about 3 percent of the population actually looks good wearing them.

Stella knew the importance of being discreet when making personal phone calls.

Glenda knew that getting Hal the new Harley Lawn-Pro would be just the motivation he needed to keep the lawn well mowed.

Hoping to induce phone calls from potential dates, Noreen performs an ancient tribal telephone dance.

Though he was a star on the school's soccer team, Les Babko was having a tough time with baseball.

"Our donations have doubled since we had that thing installed!"

"I am waxing the car! What does it *look* like I'm doing?"

"The coffeemaker is broken."

"In the last couple of months, we've noticed a big improvement in her motor skills."

"Darlene, what a clever gift idea! A dress shirt made entirely out of bread wrapper twist ties! You can wear it to your big meeting on Friday, Wayne!"

"It helps me to unwind."

"Go!"

"It only takes me about four minutes to paint the entire house, but it's a pain in the neck cleaning this thing when I'm done."

"Have you got that toilet unplugged yet?!"

REST ROOM USAGE			
EMPLOYEE	TRIPS TODAY	MONTHLY TOTAL	AVG. LENGTH OF STAY
CLARK	3	47	2 min.
FRAWLEY	6	52	4.6 min.
PATERSON	2	29	3.1 min.
MORRISON	0	4	.2 min.
MIELKE	19	33	12 min.
ROBB	13	102	34 min.
LEONARD	9	73	17 min.

Management felt that the new chart was helpful in detecting employees who were abusing rest room privileges.

"This playpen is good up to age 14!"

"You know, they always say that 80 percent of all accidents happen at home."

"I'll take a large pizza with half-onion,
two-thirds olives, nine-fifteenths mushrooms,
five-eighths pepperoni, one-eighth anchovies, and
extra cheese on five-ninths of the onion half."

Bob Swilnard was a lifeguard with an attitude.

"Whatever happened to the days when you could just tie an old tire to a tree branch?"

"We need to do something about this wax buildup."

"I hate it when it's Ohler's turn to drive."

"Dan backed over the stroller in the driveway."

**Chuck wasn't about to let another ground ball
roll through his legs.**

"That settles it! Next car we buy
has to have cloth seats!"

"I think it's time we had a little talk with
Nurse Dunn."

"I don't care if the camp got an incredible deal on this thing by buying it secondhand from Wacky World. It still gives me the creeps."

Most newlyweds have a tendency to try to avoid any conflicts.

"Maybe our price is too high."

Working for the No. 1 manufacturer of bean bag chairs does have its downside.

"Bill! We've got a problem in here with the spin cycle!!"

"We're trying to streamline things around here."

"I figured out that 478 times around the table is a mile."

"Check it out. I've been cutting a half-inch off Dad's chair legs every day for the last two weeks."

"Somebody finally got smart and came up with an above-ground pool that's got a deep end and a shallow end."

77

Although the new office cubicles were a refreshing change, they did make it difficult to have a private conversation.

"I've been after Bob for years to have a screened porch installed. But when he showed me a cost comparison between a porch and mosquito netting, I had to agree that the netting made a lot more sense."

"My name is Ron and I'm ... I'm ... having a birthday!"

"Let's see now, Helen. You're here for what? A tummy tuck? No, here it is. A face-lift."

"It gets 169 miles per gallon, but it's sort of a pain when it comes to dating and getting groceries."

"Wow! I haven't heard Dad scream that loud since we carved our names into the hood of his Corvette!"

"How's Drew doing? Is he still up?"

"All right, Dad! Now try *four* meatballs!"

At a track meet in New Jersey.

"This one is the basic cable box, this one is for upgraded service, then we've got **HBO** with this box, this one is for the 24-hour fly-fishing channel, and then of course the Vegetarian Channel, the Monster Truck channel. ..."

A behind-the-scenes look at people who
pair up college roommates.

"Freshwater pearls? No! These are
the kids' baby teeth!"

"Most people find this hole particularly challenging."

"I want an action-adventure film, she wants a romantic comedy.
I just don't see how we can resolve this!"

Obviously, Carol needed more than simply dinner out to give her a break from taking care of her four kids.

"Watch your step. There's quite a drop-off over here."

Mrs. Mutner liked to go over a few of her rules
on the first day of school.

"Sorry about the mix-up with the keyboards. We hope this won't affect your programming abilities."

"He does not have a discipline problem! He's just had a little too much sugar, that's all."

89

"I have to give myself a lot of the blame.
I gave Dave a book called *How to Build Your
Own Deck* for Father's Day."

"I had to do 95 the whole way back on the interstate,
but I got Darla home by midnight like you wanted,
Mr. Lampley."

"This is my new recycling system."

"Hey! Can they do that?!"

The downside of going on a two-week vacation.

"Good morning, and welcome to
The Wonders of Physics."

"For the last time, no, you may not have
your own phone for the backseat!"

Frank and Vern would go to any length to
get the free lunch deal.

"We're having a little trouble with our scanners. Just divide our total by 37.21."

"According to this scale, I've lost seven pounds just from walking around the carnival!"

"I want to apologize to all of you for the side effects caused by last week's lab."

"This just seemed to make a lot more sense. Now we just take out the mail we want and leave the rest."

"I've been bugging Roger forever to have central air conditioning installed, but he insists that we don't need it."

"Ready to *work* at 8 o'clock, Velez! Not just *here* at 8 o'clock! Ready to work!"

"That's another great thing about having a sunroof!
It gives us the ability to fit into much
tighter parking spots!"

How to tell when it's time to wash your gym socks.

A lot of people feel that the personalized-check rage is getting out of hand.

"How ironic! You walk 9 miles in 90 degree heat to borrow some coat hangers, struggle for $2\frac{1}{2}$ hours to open the door, and here I've had a spare set of keys in my purse the whole time!"

"Yep, this is definitely a record! 139 inches! It beats the creamed corn back on August 14 by 6½ inches."

Although they did help to boost attendance at tournaments, the PGA cheerleaders were eventually banned from the tour after repeated complaints from players.

"Psycho? He's a Pekingese. This is all just for effect to ward off burglars!"

"Let's see now ... driver's license, driver's license ... could you hold this, too? Driver's license, driver's license ... describe it to me again. ..."

The latest in couch-potato technology: the gas-powered recliner.

"If there's anything Ray can't stand it's raking leaves."

"I had it installed to discourage tailgaters."

"I think I found the problem. We left out a period."

"He cost a thousand bucks, but he's one of a rare breed that knows how to empty its own litter box."

"My Uncle Leon left us his Elvis chair and matching lamp."

"When I got done, I discovered there had been a cockroach on the sunlamp the whole time."

109

"In case you haven't noticed, the Milligans got one of those leaf blowers."

"That's the beauty of it! To your average burglar they look like real kids. But they're actually just ceramic dummies with a slot in the bottom for hiding spare house keys."

"They're done! HA HA! *All* the school lunches are done for the next 186 days!
No more getting up at 6 a.m.! No more messy sandwiches! No more. ..."

"She's a little cranky when she's tired."

"Jeepers! Is it 12:25 already? A half-hour just isn't enough time for lunch, is it?"

"But the feature that *really* sold us on this vacuum cleaner was its personal hygiene attachments!"

Let's face it. Everybody does this when they're assigned a 2,000-word term paper.

"And this is our most popular sofa bed, which we call our 'On the Road Again' model. After two consecutive days of use as a bed, it begins to emit a hideous odor that inevitably persuades tiresome guests to hit the road."

Research has shown that wearing a baseball cap backward lowers one's IQ by as much as 50 points.

A hot new fad: the party skateboard.

"I've been saving us a bundle by buying in bulk!"

Lloyd Finster was having a tough time adjusting to life as a retiree.

"I don't mean to criticize, but you put those nonslip decals in the tub upside down."

"For Pete's sake, will you take that ridiculous wig off her?! It is perfectly normal for a 6-month-old to have no hair!"

Friends of the Norblocks were beginning to sense some tension between Ed and Helen.

"What am I doing? I'm making this two-pronged outlet into a three-pronged outlet."

"I *told* you it was a stupid idea to buy contact lenses at a rummage sale!"

"... and one for you!"

"I tell ya, meals used to be such a pain in the neck! Now, thanks to the vending machines, they're a breeze. No more cooking, no more dirty dishes. ..."

"Personally, I think this new reorganization plan stinks."

"I think you've made your point!"

"Oh, for heaven's sake! Don't tell me you were racing against the electric garage-door opener again!"

"Ryan's walking two months earlier than most other kids, thanks to these training shoes that Gary made in the basement."

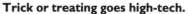

Trick or treating goes high-tech.

"He's got such interesting markings!"

Coach Wazler discovered that attaching likenesses of players' mothers-in-law to the blocking sled is a powerful motivational tool.

The new coffee distribution system not only
boosted morale, but it also cut down on time spent
mindlessly lingering around the coffee machine.

"Here you go, right on page 13 of the manual:
'Never stop walking while the treadmill is on.'"